BERNIE SANDERS

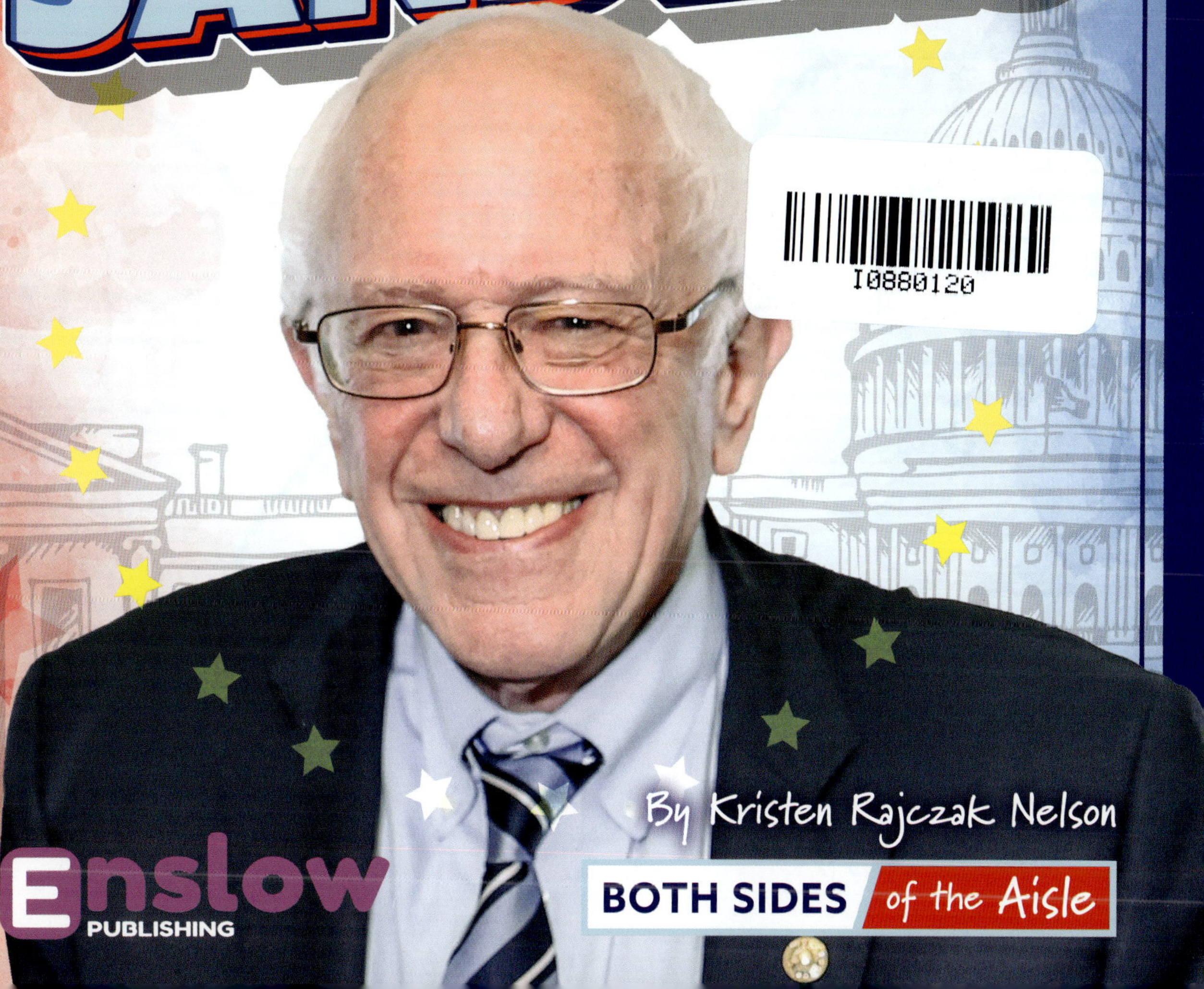

By Kristen Rajczak Nelson

BOTH SIDES of the Aisle

Enslow PUBLISHING

Please visit our website, www.enslow.com. For a free color catalog of all our high-quality books, call toll free 1-800-398-2504 or fax 1-877-980-4454.

Library of Congress Cataloging-in-Publication Data

Names: Rajczak Nelson, Kristen author
Title: Bernie Sanders / Kristen Rajczak Nelson.
Description: Buffalo, New York : Enslow Publishing, [2026] | Series: Both sides of the aisle | Includes bibliographical references and index. | Audience: Grades 2-3
Identifiers: LCCN 2025021613 (print) | LCCN 2025021614 (ebook) | ISBN 9781978546547 library binding | ISBN 9781978546530 paperback | ISBN 9781978546554 ebook
Subjects: LCSH: Sanders, Bernard–Juvenile literature | United States. Congress. Senate–Biography–Juvenile literature | United States. Congress. House–Biography–Juvenile literature | Legislators–United States–Biography–Juvenile literature | Legislators–Vermont–Biography–Juvenile literature | Vermont–Biography–Juvenile literature | LCGFT: Biographies
Classification: LCC E840.8.S26 R34 2026 (print) | LCC E840.8.S26 (ebook) | DDC 328.743092 [B]–dc23/eng/20250716
LC record available at https://lccn.loc.gov/2025021613
LC ebook record available at https://lccn.loc.gov/2025021614

Published in 2026 by
Enslow Publishing
2544 Clinton Street
Buffalo, NY 14224

Designer: Andrea Davison-Bartolotta
Editor: Therese Shea

Photo credits: Cover, p. 1 (main) Palácio do Planalto/Flickr.com; cover, p. 1 (buildings) Fandorina Liza/Shutterstock.com; series art (background stars) v_kulieva/Shutterstock.com; series art (watercolor background) Apostrophe/Shutterstock.com; p. 5 lev radin/Shutterstock.com; p. 7 (inset) File:Bernie Sanders 1959 High School Yearbook.jpg/Wikimedia Commons; p. 7 (main) Roland Marconi/Shutterstock.com; p. 9 Everett Collection/Shutterstock.com; p. 11 Maxim Elramsisy/Shutterstock.com; p. 13 Donna Light/Associated Press; p. 15 Joseph Sohm/Shutterstock.com; p. 17 Gordon Donovan/Shutterstock.com; p. 19 Gino Santa Maria/Shutterstock.com; p. 20 Sheila Fitzgerald/Shutterstock.com.

Printed in the United States of America

CPSIA compliance information: Batch #CWENS26: For further information contact Enslow Publishing, at 1-800-398-2504.

CONTENTS

Words in the glossary appear in **bold** type the first time they are used in the text.

WHAT SANDERS STANDS FOR

In 1997, Bernie Sanders put out the book *Outsider in the White House*. In it, he wrote about the U.S. economic gap: "There is something **profoundly** wrong when the top one-tenth of 1 percent [of Americans] owns almost as much as the bottom 90 percent." That means a few people own much of the nation's wealth.

Today, this idea remains central to Sanders as a member of the U.S. Senate. His work and life **experiences** have allowed him to make a special connection to many Americans.

MORE TO KNOW

Economic means having to do with the economy. The economy is the money made in an area and how it is made.

Sanders is known for his grassroots campaigns. This means having regular people taking part in spreading the word about something instead of a big company or group.

BROOKLYN BORN

Bernard Sanders was born on September 8, 1941, in Brooklyn, which is part of New York City. His father, Eli, came to the United States from Poland in 1921. Sanders's mother, Dorothy, was born in New York City. Sanders grew up with an older brother named Larry.

Sanders's father sold paint. He worked hard. However, the Sanders family never had much money. Right after Sanders finished high school, his mother died. Just two years later, his father passed away.

MORE TO KNOW

Sanders has said his father "had unbelievable courage in journeying across an ocean, with no money in his pocket and not knowing a word of English."

SANDERS - 1959

Sanders's childhood, especially the family's lack of extra money, had a great effect on his views later in life.

GETTING INTO POLITICS

Sanders first went to Brooklyn College. Then, he went to the University of Chicago where he studied **political science**. He graduated, or finished his classes, in 1964.

While in college, Sanders took part in the civil rights movement. In fact, he attended the March on Washington for Jobs and Freedom in 1963 with 200,000 other Americans. This march **protested** the treatment of Black Americans and **supported** civil rights laws in Congress.

MORE TO **KNOW**

The civil rights movement was a time in U.S. history starting in the 1950s in which Black Americans fought for equal civil rights, or the freedoms granted to us by law.

The March on Washington is remembered today as the event at which Dr. Martin Luther King Jr. gave his famous "I Have a Dream…" speech. Sanders was there to hear it!

FINDING HIS WAY

Sanders lived in Israel for a short time after college. He then moved to Vermont. He didn't have a steady job for a while. He wrote articles and worked a bit as a carpenter. Sanders joined a political group that was against the Vietnam War too.

Sanders became a leader in the group. He began running for office. He ran for governor of Vermont in 1972 and 1976—and lost. He ran for U.S. Senate in 1972 and 1974—and lost.

MORE TO **KNOW**

The Vietnam War was a conflict starting in 1955 and ending in 1975 between South Vietnam and North Vietnam in which the United States supported South Vietnam.

The political group Sanders joined was called Liberty Union. It aimed to end the war in Vietnam as well as disrupt, or upset, the two main **political parties**.

MAYOR SANDERS

In 1981, Sanders ran for mayor of Burlington. This is the city in Vermont that has the most people. Some supporters remember that he didn't look like a normal politician. Sanders didn't even own a tie! He spoke out about local issues, or problems, such as the high cost of **utilities**. Sanders won the **election** by only 10 votes.

As mayor, Sanders worked hard to make life better for everyone in Burlington. The people reelected him three more times!

MORE TO **KNOW**

Before becoming mayor, Sanders made a documentary, or factual movie, about Eugene Debs, a man who ran for president outside of the main political parties in 1920.

Sanders ran for mayor as an independent. That means he was not part of a political party, such as the Democratic or Republican Party.

IN CONGRESS

In 1990, Sanders was elected to the U.S. House of **Representatives**. Sanders served 16 years in the House as a representative from Vermont. During that time, he co-founded the Congressional Progressive Caucus (CPC).

In 2006, Sanders was elected to the Senate. He was reelected in 2012, 2018, and 2024. He has been part of many Senate committees, or groups, including the **budget** committee. In this group, Sanders fights against big companies trying to make money in ways that hurt others.

MORE TO **KNOW**

The CPC fights for economic equality, civil rights, and health care for all, among other issues.

Vermont is one of the smallest states in the country. Sanders served as the only representative in the House for his state.

STILL INDEPENDENT

While serving in both the House and Senate, Sanders has remained an independent. He describes himself as a "democratic socialist." Sanders says democratic socialism means that people should work to change our political system for the better and make the economy work for every person, not just those who have a lot of money.

However, Sanders's interests often line up with the Democrats in the Senate. He has often voted with them. In 2016, Sanders tried to connect with the Democrats even more.

MORE TO KNOW

Sanders is the longest serving independent in Congress's history!

After winning the 2024 Senate election, Sanders thanked the people of Vermont. He said, "It is the honor of my life to represent you."

RUNNING FOR PRESIDENT

Sanders worked to earn the Democratic **nomination** for president in 2016. Many people didn't think he could win against Hillary Clinton. They were right—but not before Sanders became a household name and his ideas brought in many supporters.

Sanders especially excited young Democrats with his plans if he were elected: health care for all, free **tuition** to public colleges and universities, and tax increases for the rich. His ideas helped shape the Democratic Party after that election.

MORE TO KNOW

Sanders ran for president again in 2020. He lost the Democratic nomination to Joe Biden, who went on to become president.

Sanders wrote a book after his bid for president in 2016, *Our Revolution: A Future to Believe In*. Sanders has written other books about his life and politics too.

Sanders Speaks Up!

Sanders has been an important voice in American politics, especially in the last decade. He continues to stand for the people of Vermont as well as support laws that close the economic gap between the rich and average Americans.

Sanders is well known as a fiery and moving speaker. Even as he moves through his 80s, the young civil rights and anti-war **activist** he was still shines through. There's no doubt that Sanders will continue to voice his beliefs and speak up against inequality.

BERNIE SANDERS TIMELINE

1941	Sanders is born in Brooklyn, New York.
1964	He graduates from the University of Chicago.
1981	He is elected mayor of Burlington, Vermont. He serves until 1989.
1991	He begins to serve in the U.S. House of Representatives. He serves until 2007.
2007	He begins to serve in the U.S. Senate.
2016	He tries to earn the Democratic nomination for president but does not.
2020	He tries to earn the Democratic nomination for president but does not.
2024	He is elected to a fourth term in the U.S. Senate.

Sanders has been making a difference in American politics for decades.

MORE TO KNOW

When Sanders isn't working in Washington, DC, he lives in Burlington with his wife, Jane. They have four children and seven grandchildren.

GLOSSARY

activist: A person who uses or supports strong actions to help make changes in politics or society.

budget: A plan for the spending of money.

election: The act of electing, or voting someone into a government position.

experience: Something a person has gone through.

nomination: The act of nominating, or choosing someone to be a candidate for office.

political party: A group of people with similar beliefs about how a government should be run.

political science: The study of politics, or the activities of the government and government officials.

profoundly: Very.

protest: To strongly oppose something.

representative: A member of a lawmaking body who acts for voters.

support: To hold up or to help.

tuition: The amount one must pay to go to a school.

utility: A service such as water, light, or power.

FOR MORE INFORMATION

Books

Fleischer, Jeff. *Votes of Confidence: A Young Person's Guide to American Elections*. Minneapolis, MN: Zest Books, 2024.

Yacka, Douglas. *What Is a Presidential Election?* New York, NY: Penguin Workshop, 2024.

Websites

Bernie Sanders Official Website
berniesanders.com
Stay up-to-date with what Sanders is up to on his website.

Senator Bernie Sanders
www.sanders.senate.gov
Check out Sanders's Senate website for more information.

Publisher's note to educators and parents: Our editors have carefully reviewed these websites to ensure that they are suitable for students. Many websites change frequently, however, and we cannot guarantee that a site's future contents will continue to meet our high standards of quality and educational value. Be advised that students should be closely supervised whenever they access the internet.

INDEX